VANISHING
at
LACDA

Images by

Wally Gilbert

An Exhibition at the

Los Angeles Center
for Digital Art

107 West Fifth Street
Los Angeles, CA 90013
December 10, 2009 –January 2, 2010
Opening Reception: December 10, 2009, 7 pm – 9 pm

Wednesday – Saturday, 12 pm – 5 pm
www.lacda.com
lacda@lacda.com
tel. 323-646-9427

Catalogue of Images

8

WALLY GILBERT: VANISHING

Nobel Laureate Wally Gilbert, world renowned for his work as a scientist as well as an artist, began a new direction in his work beginning with a wall sized piece named the "Vanishing Diptych" which won a Mary Schein Award at the recent Cambridge Art Association exhibit. Creating a series of abstractions that are each an ever more mysterious and complex variation on this initial image, there are 18 works in this series including a number of large scale prints to be on display for this LACDA exhibit.

The Vanishing Diptych was made by taking the silhouette of a head, converting it into an outline with a sharp outer edge and a diffuse inner edge, and then shrinking the image and superimposing it upon the original image repeatedly. The artist became interested in the textures that were produced by this process and turned many smaller areas of the original image into pictures in their own right. This practice of overlapping images and differently colored layers produced interaction and Moiré patterns as well as a large variety of brilliant colors in a purely aesthetic exploration which makes for an energetic formalistic romp.

Each variation and layer thereof is an ever more electronic 'close up' of that which was in the prior image. One gets the sense that this series reflects the influence his work as a microbiologist (and the ever deeper exploration of the layered realm of electronic imaging in his study of genetics) has had over his artwork.

Artist Photographer Wally Gilbert had a career as a Molecular Biologist. Awarded a Nobel Prize in 1980 for discovering a rapid DNA sequencing method, he is now following a new passion in creating visual art. He has had twenty-seven solo-exhibits, including an exhibit at the Massachusetts College of Art in 2004 and a major installation in both Warsaw and Lodz in 2007.

— Rex Bruce (November 2009)

Rex Bruce is the founder and director of Los Angeles Center for Digital Art.

Hangings on Canvas

Two Diptychs

98 inches by 88 inches

Vanishing Diptych

2009,
98" x 88" Archival Print on Canvas
Edition of 3

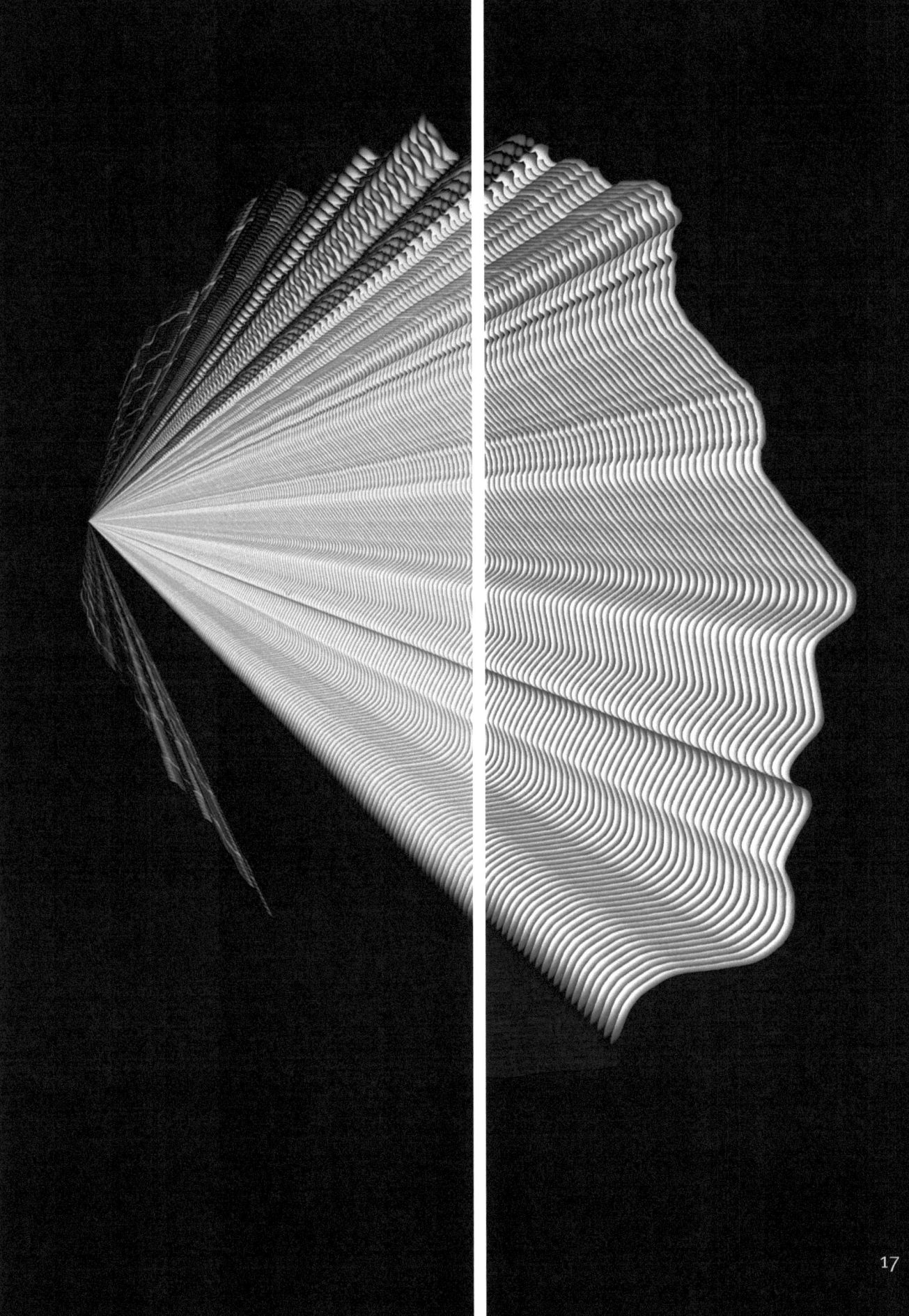

Vanishing #2 Inverse Diptych

2009,
98" x 88" Archival Print on Canvas
Edition of 3

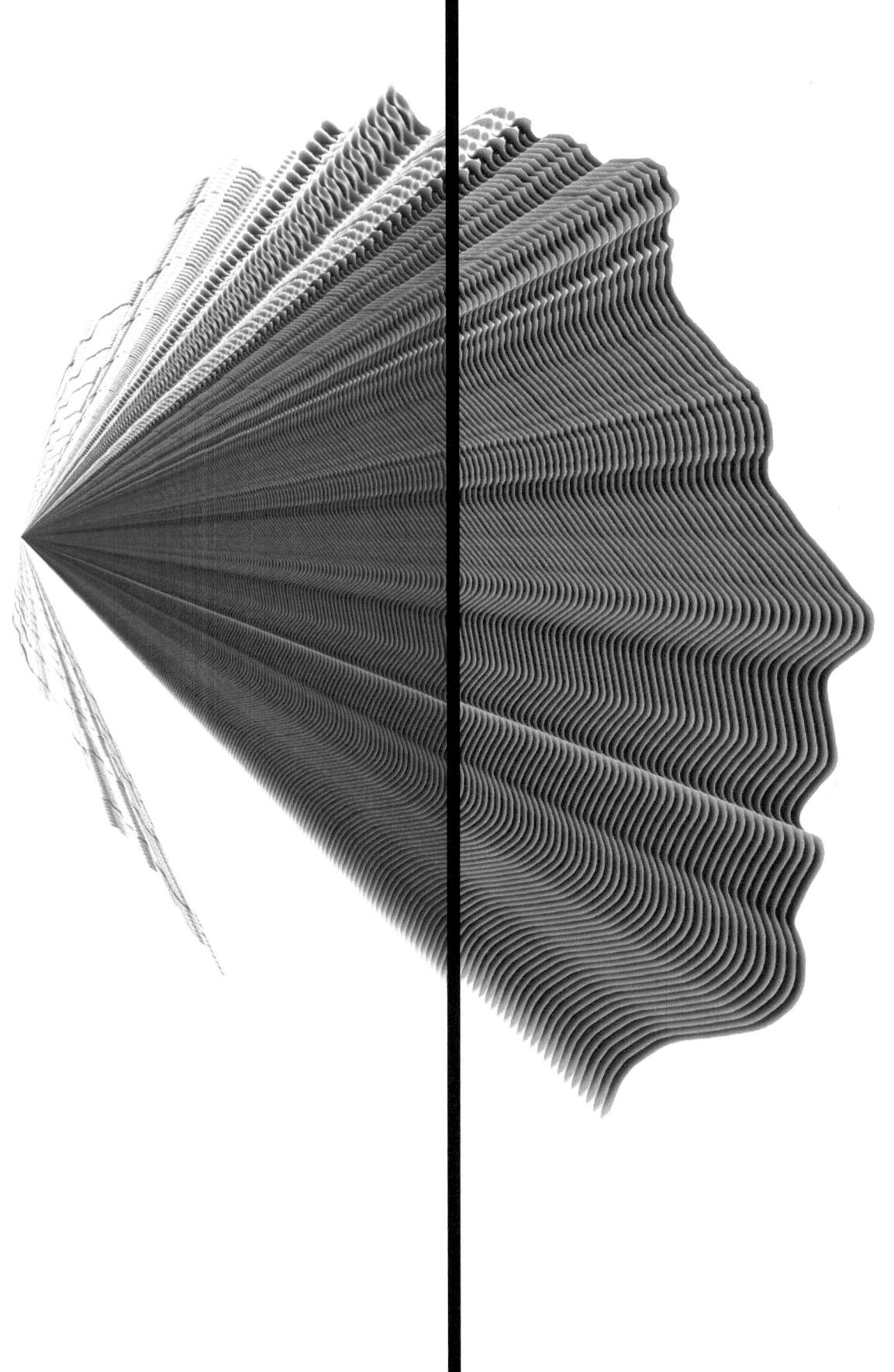

Six Hangings on Canvas

66 inches by 44 inches

Four Faces Inverse

2009,
66" x 44" Archival Print on Canvas
Edition of 3

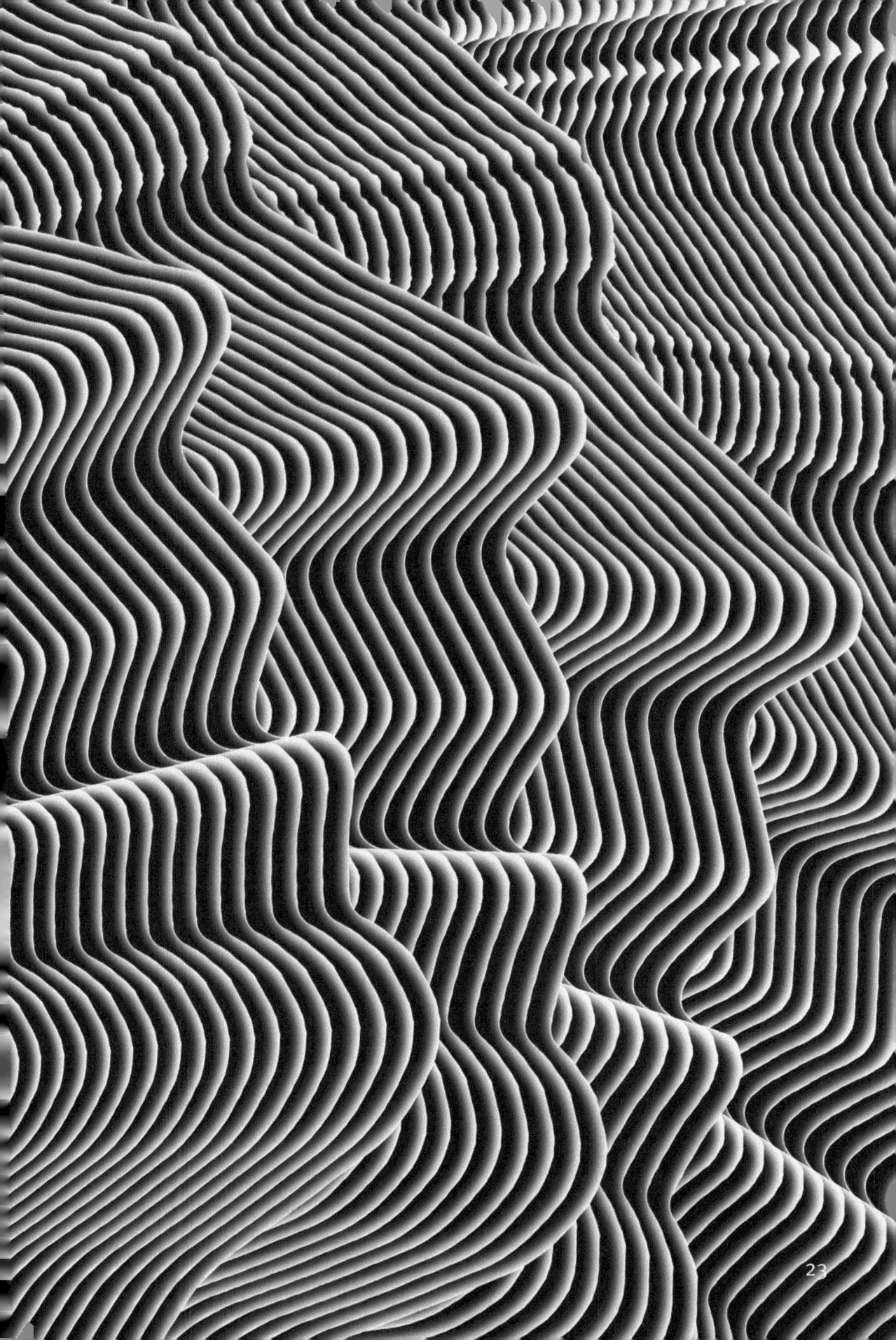

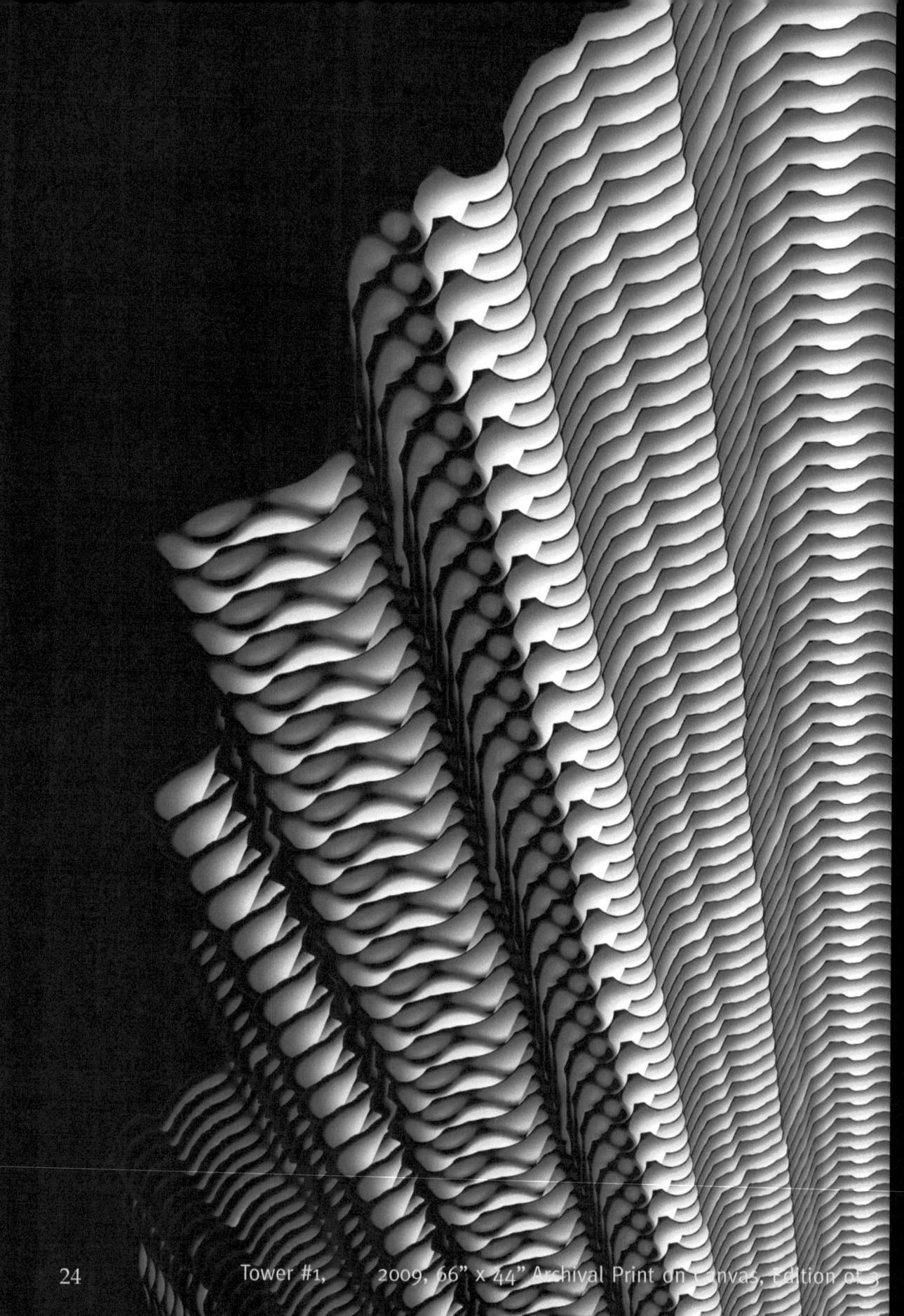

Tower #1,   2009, 66" x 44" Archival Print on Canvas, edition of 3

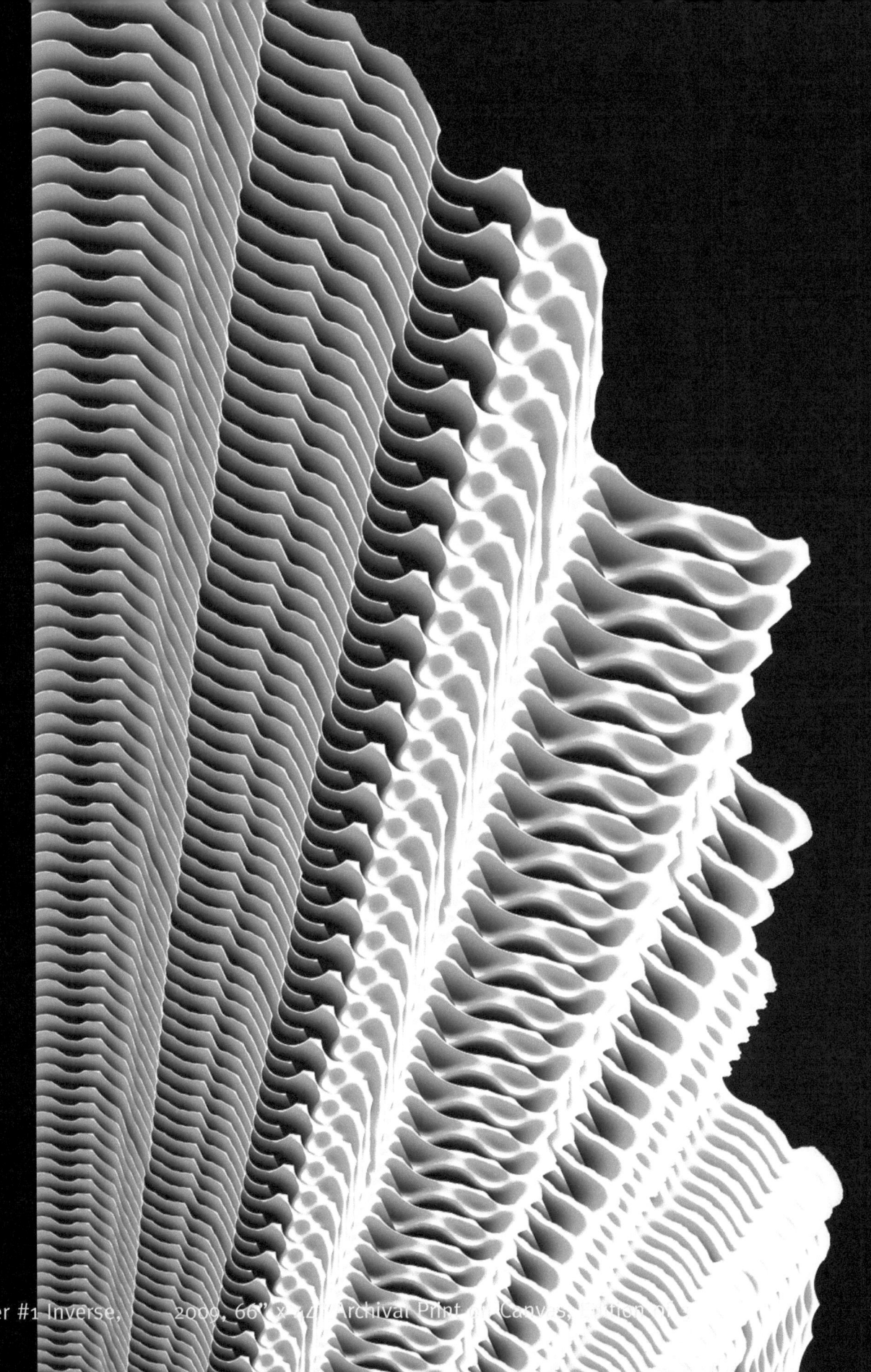

Tower #1 Inverse, 2009, 66" x 44" Archival Print on Canvas, Edition of 9

Tall Color

2009,
66" x 44" Archival Print on Canvas
Edition of 3

Red Double #2 Blur

2009,
66" x 44" Archival Print on Canvas
Edition of 3

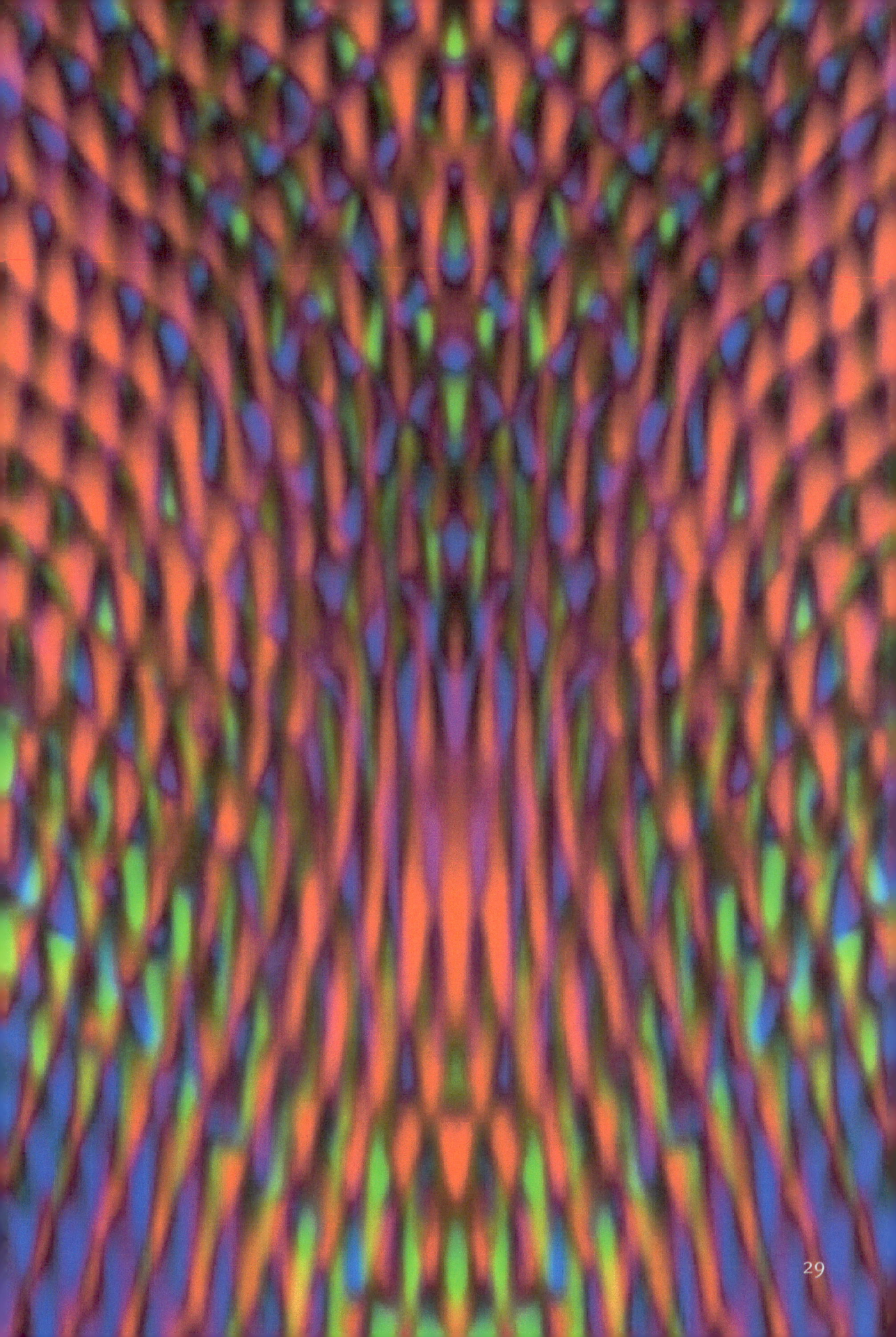

29

Blue-Green Points #2 Blur #2

2009,
66" x 44" Archival Print on Canvas
Edition of 3

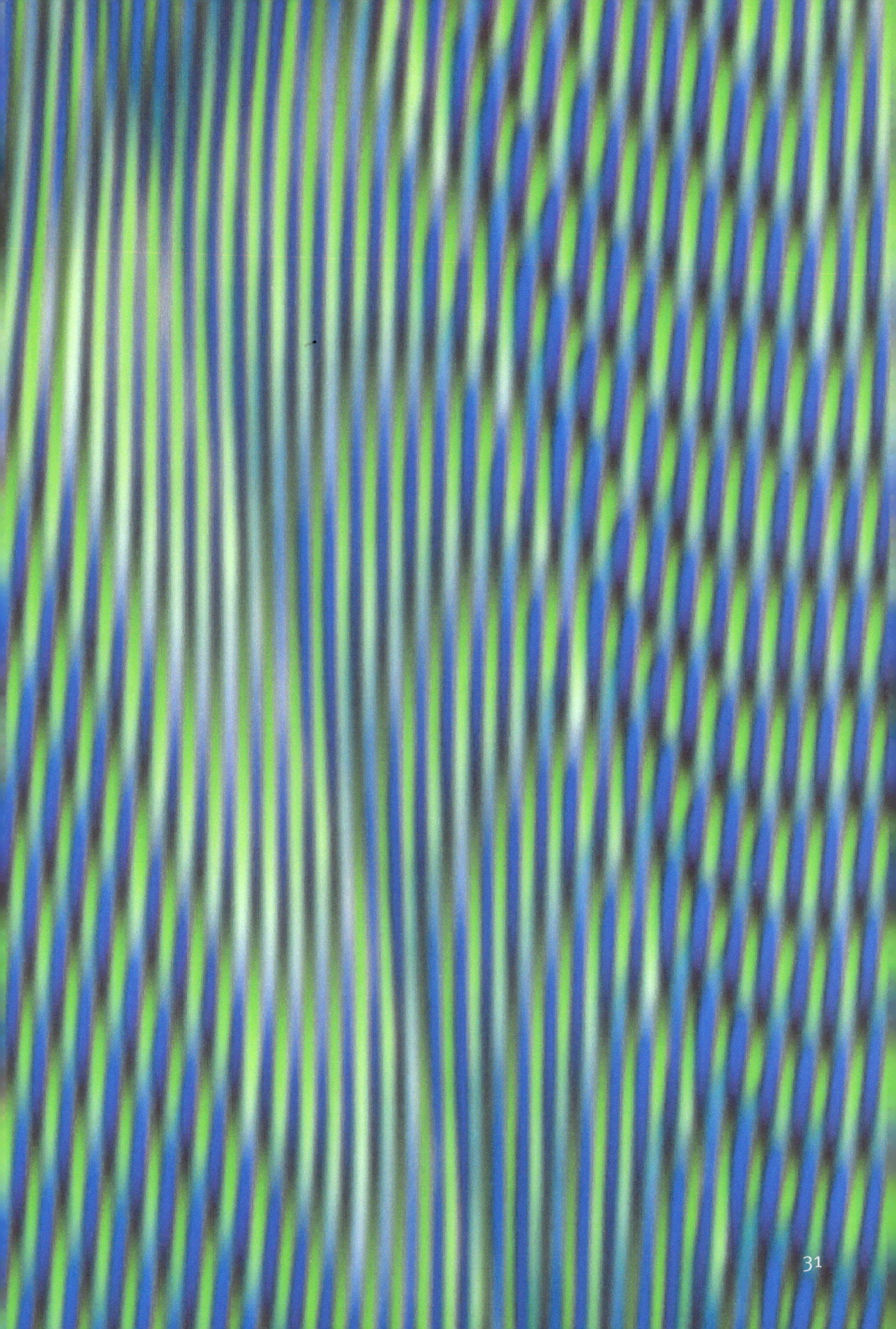

Sixteen Works on Paper

38 inches by 30 inches

on

44 inches by 36 inches paper

Four Heads Rising

2009,
38" x 30" Archival Print on 44" x 36" Satin Paper
Edition of 3

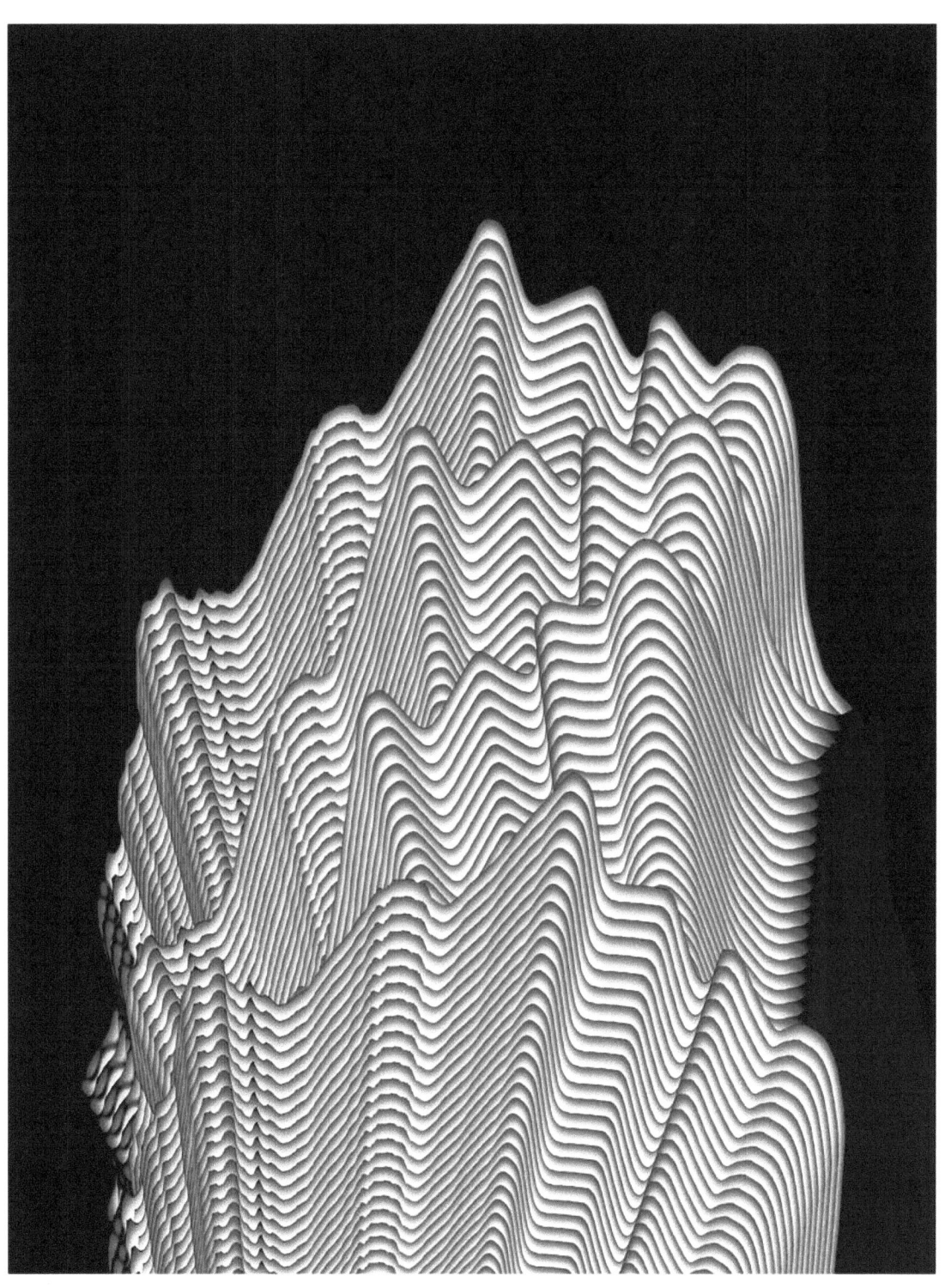

Mysterious

2009,
38" x 30" Archival Print on 44" x 36" Satin Paper
Edition of 3

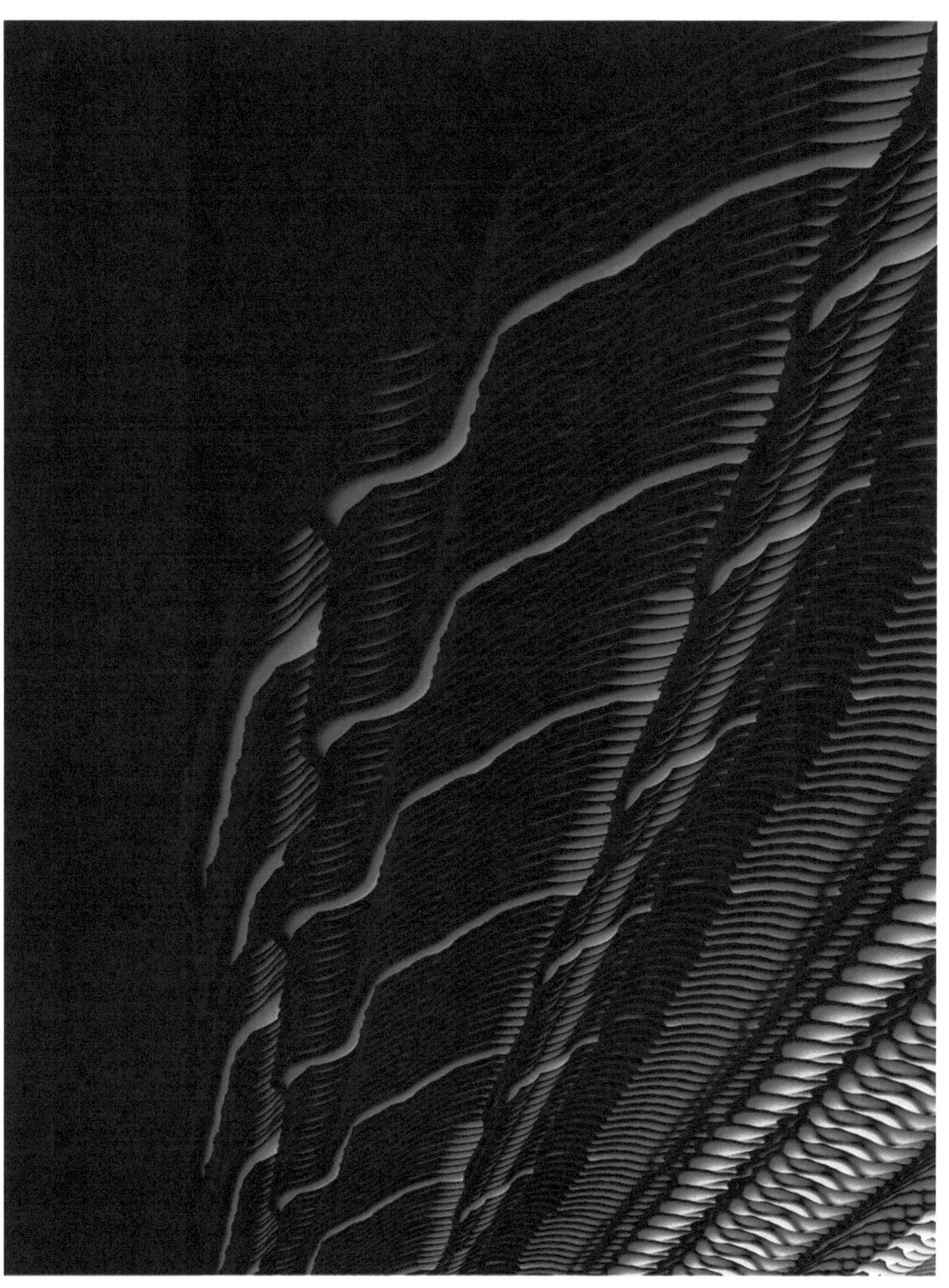

Difference #2

2009,
38" x 30" Archival Print on 44" x 36" Satin Paper
Edition of 3

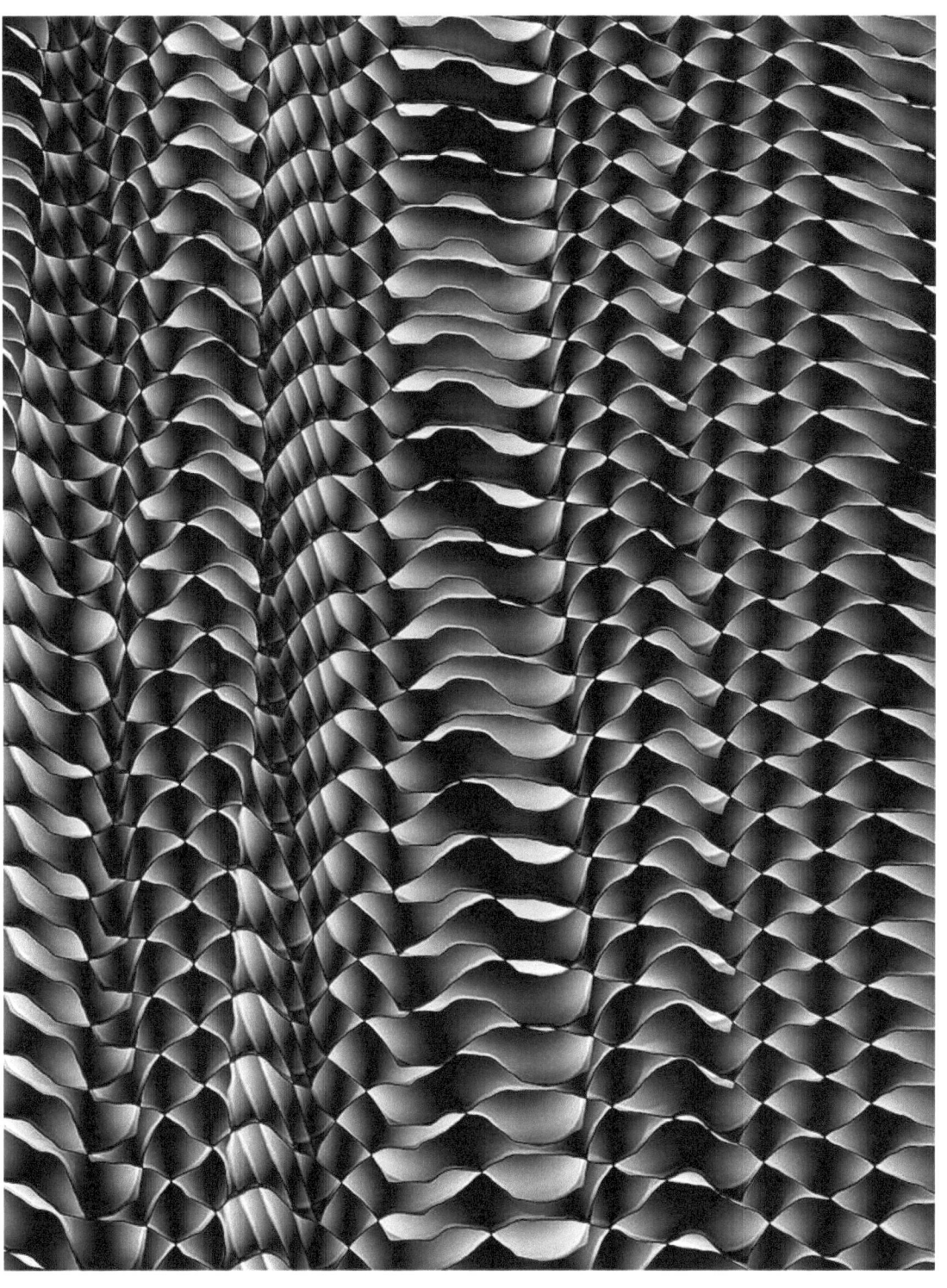

Color Bands #4A

2009,
38" x 30" Archival Print on 44" x 36" Satin Paper
Edition of 3

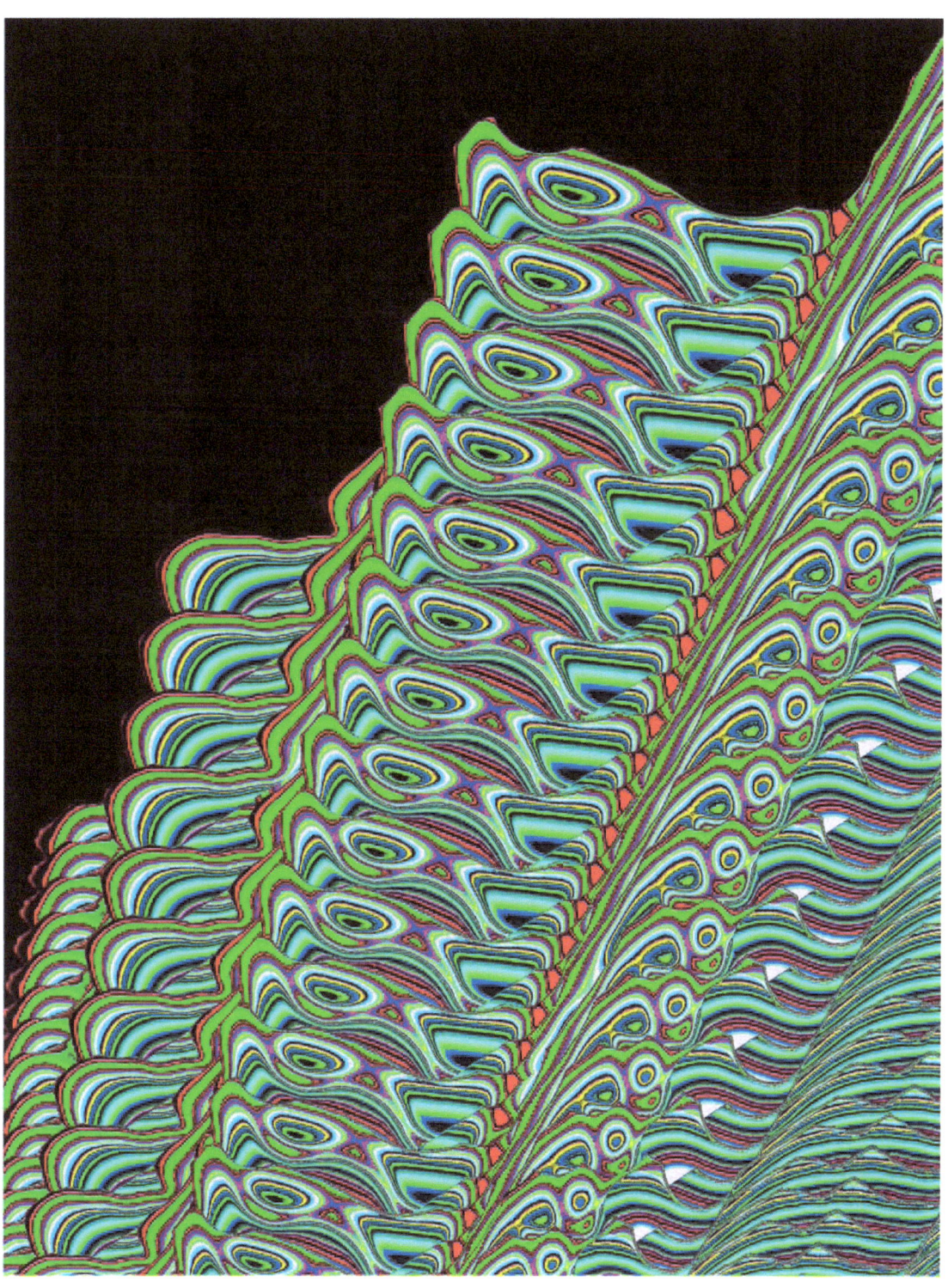

Color Bands #4B

2009,
38" x 30" Archival Print on 44" x 36" Satin Paper
Edition of 3

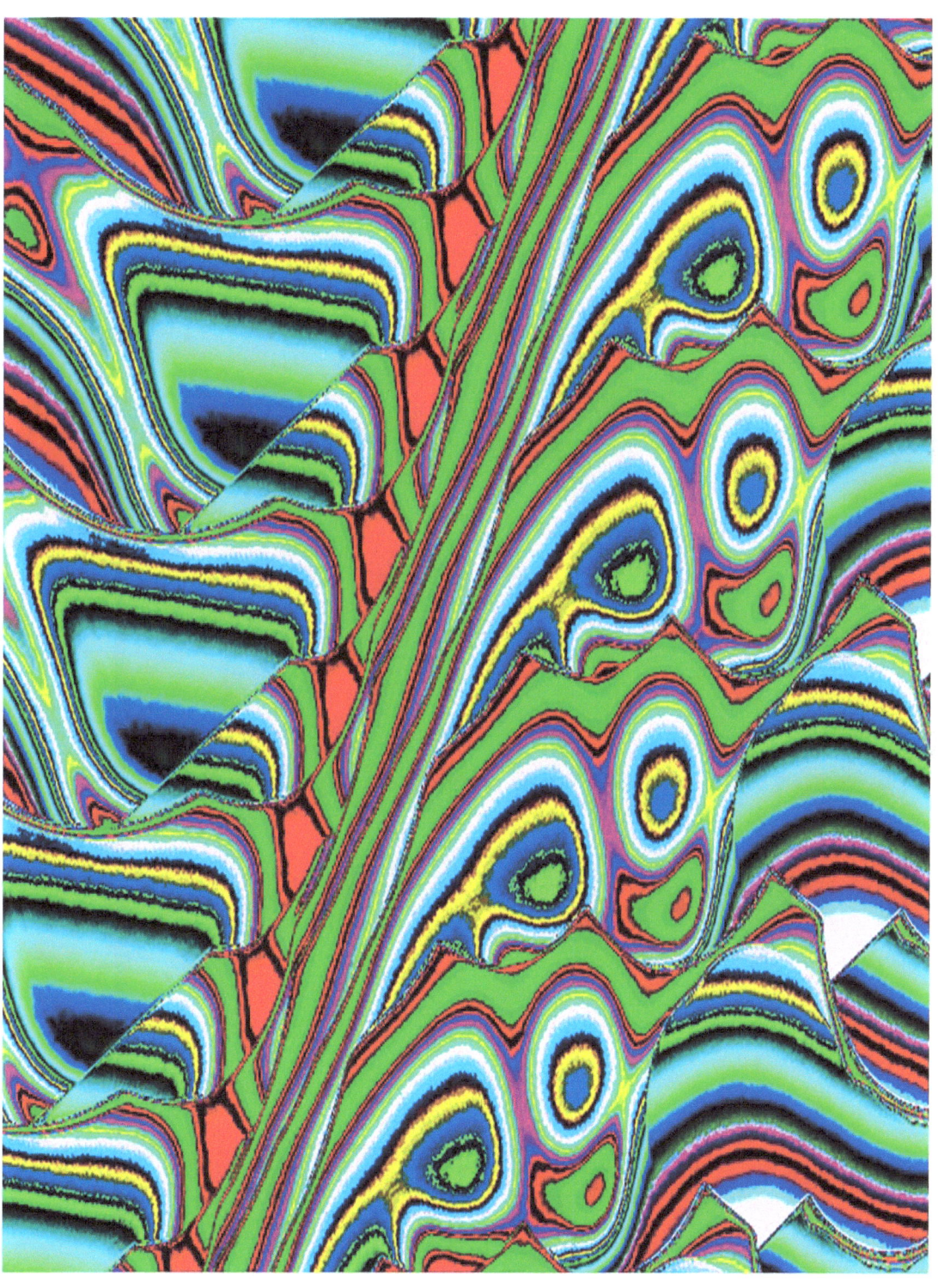

Tall

2009,
38" x 30" Archival Print on 44" x 36" Satin Paper
Edition of 3

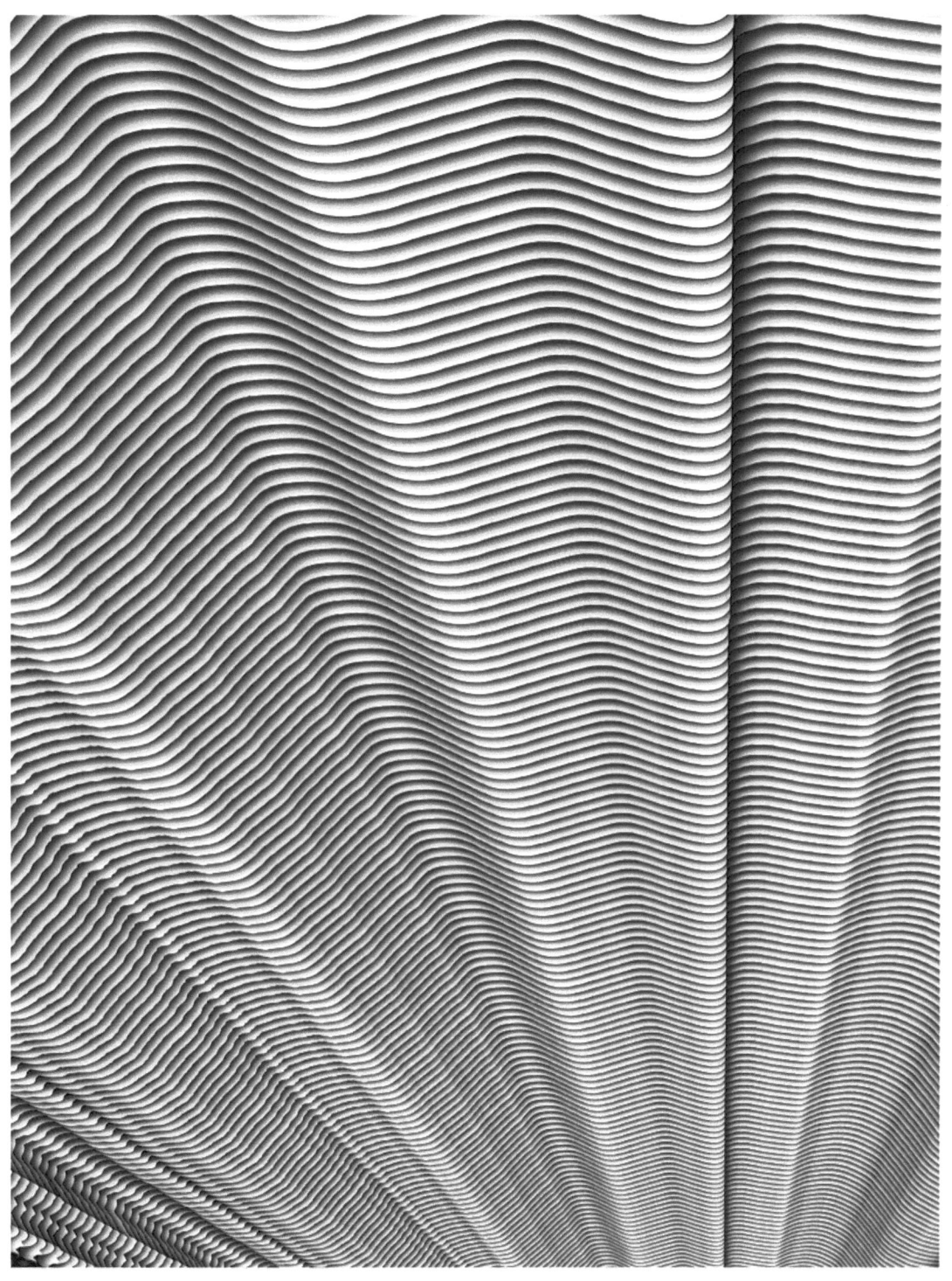

Tall Color Dip-C Blue

2009,
38" x 30" Archival Print on 44" x 36" Satin Paper
Edition of 3

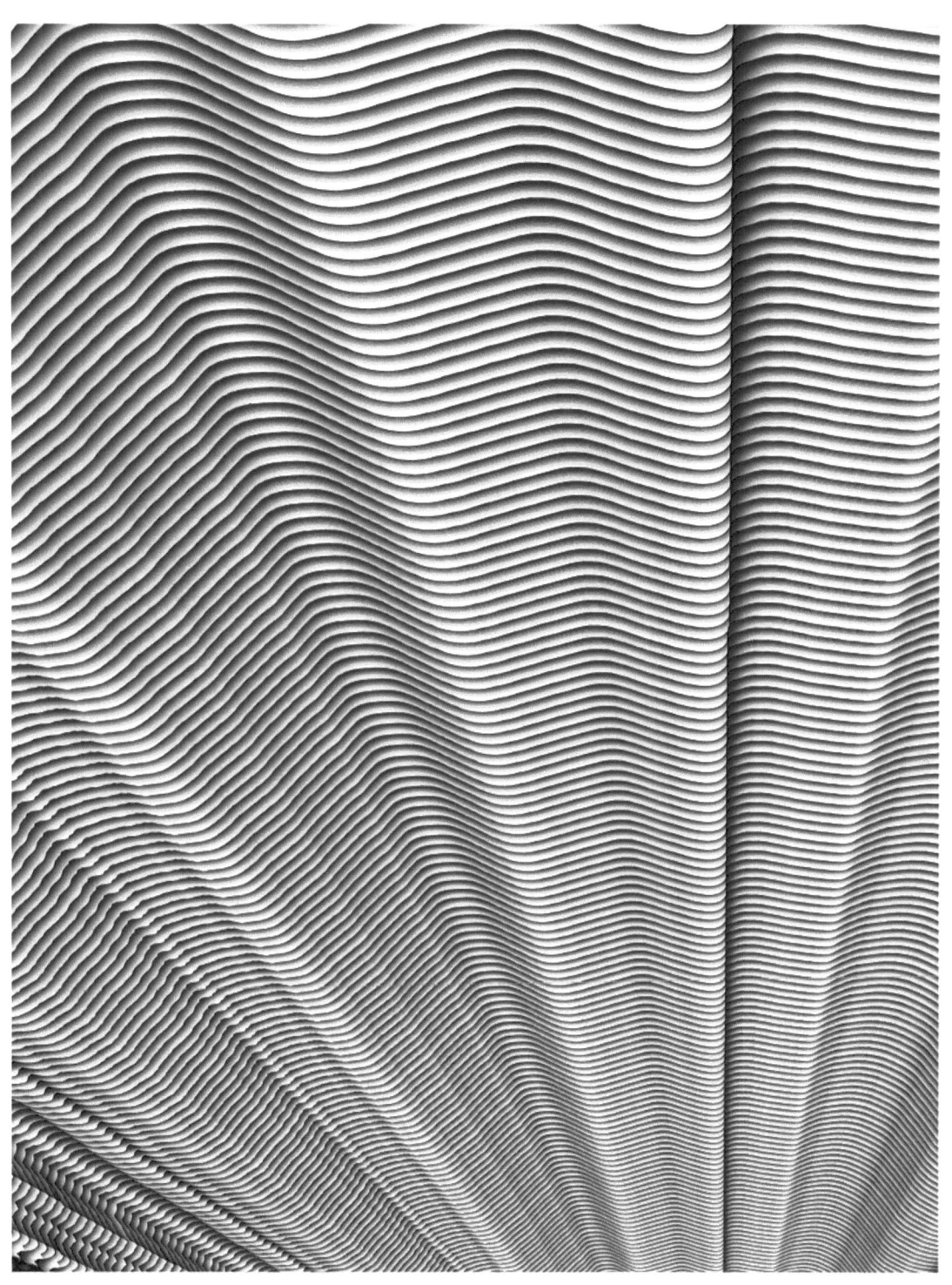

Tall Color Dip-C Blue

2009,
38" x 30" Archival Print on 44" x 36" Satin Paper
Edition of 3

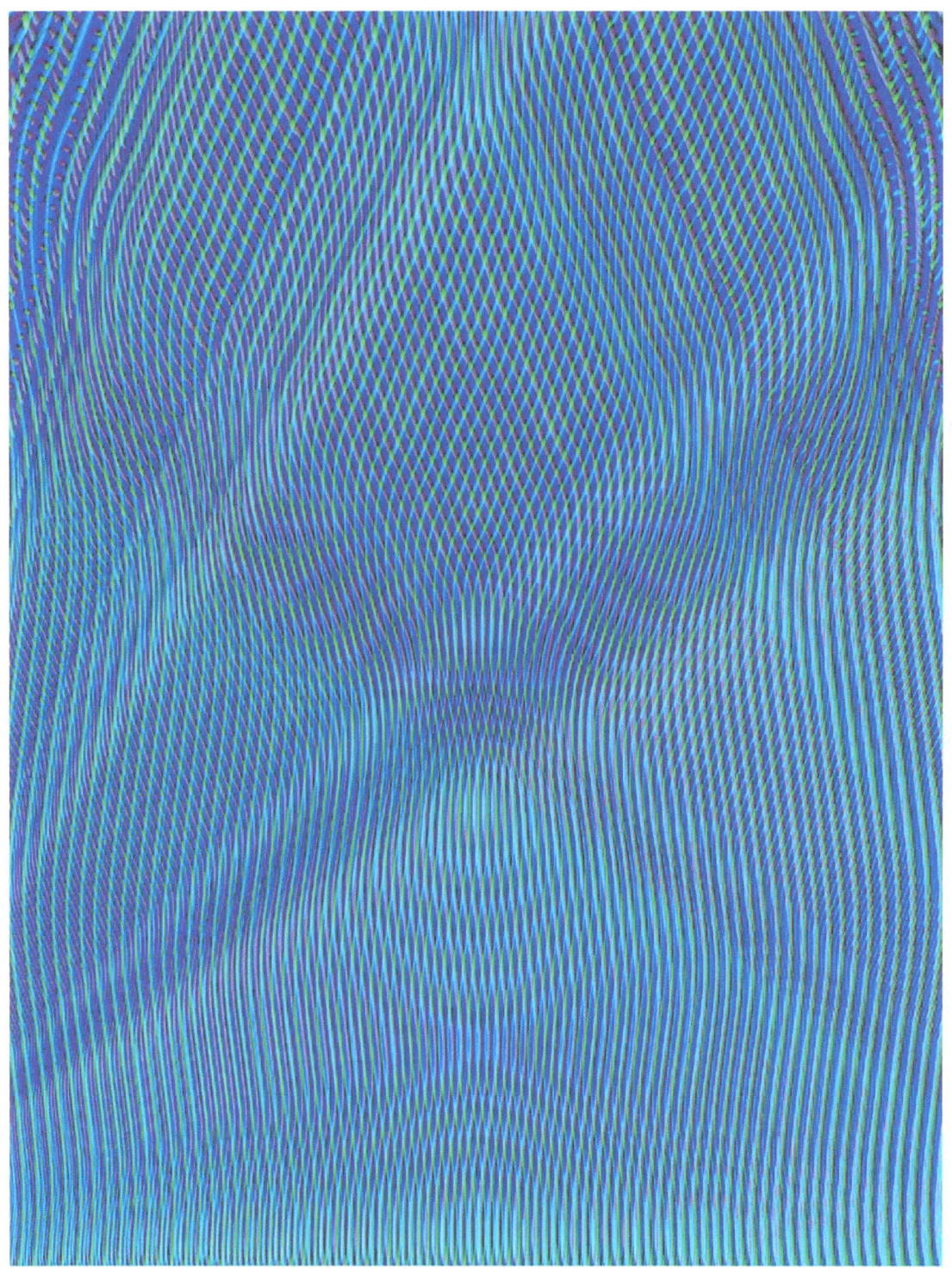

Tall Color Dip-D Yellow-Red

2009,
38" x 30" Archival Print on 44" x 36" Satin Paper
Edition of 3

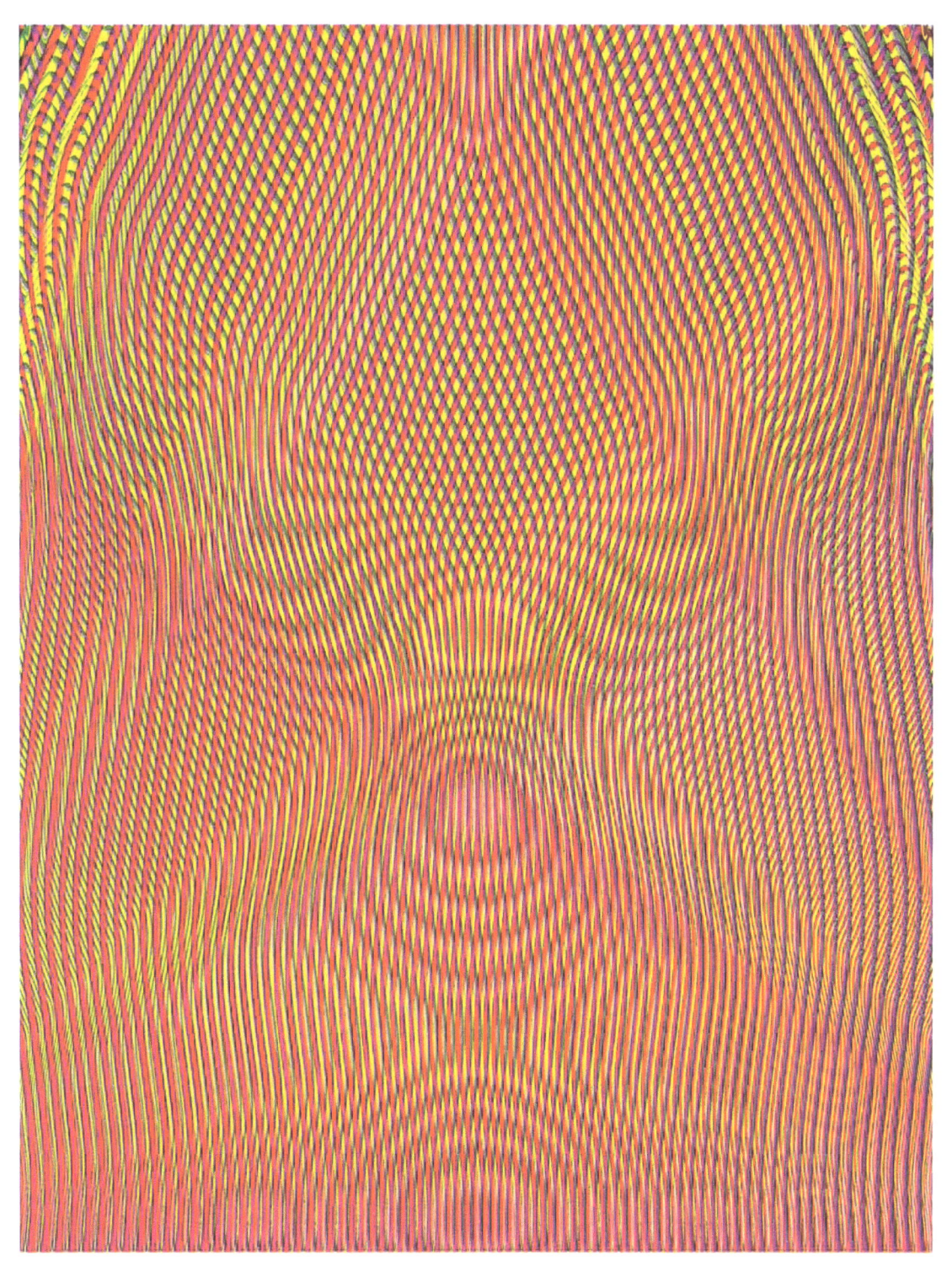

Tall Tilted

2009,
38" x 30" Archival Print on 44" x 36" Satin Paper
Edition of 3

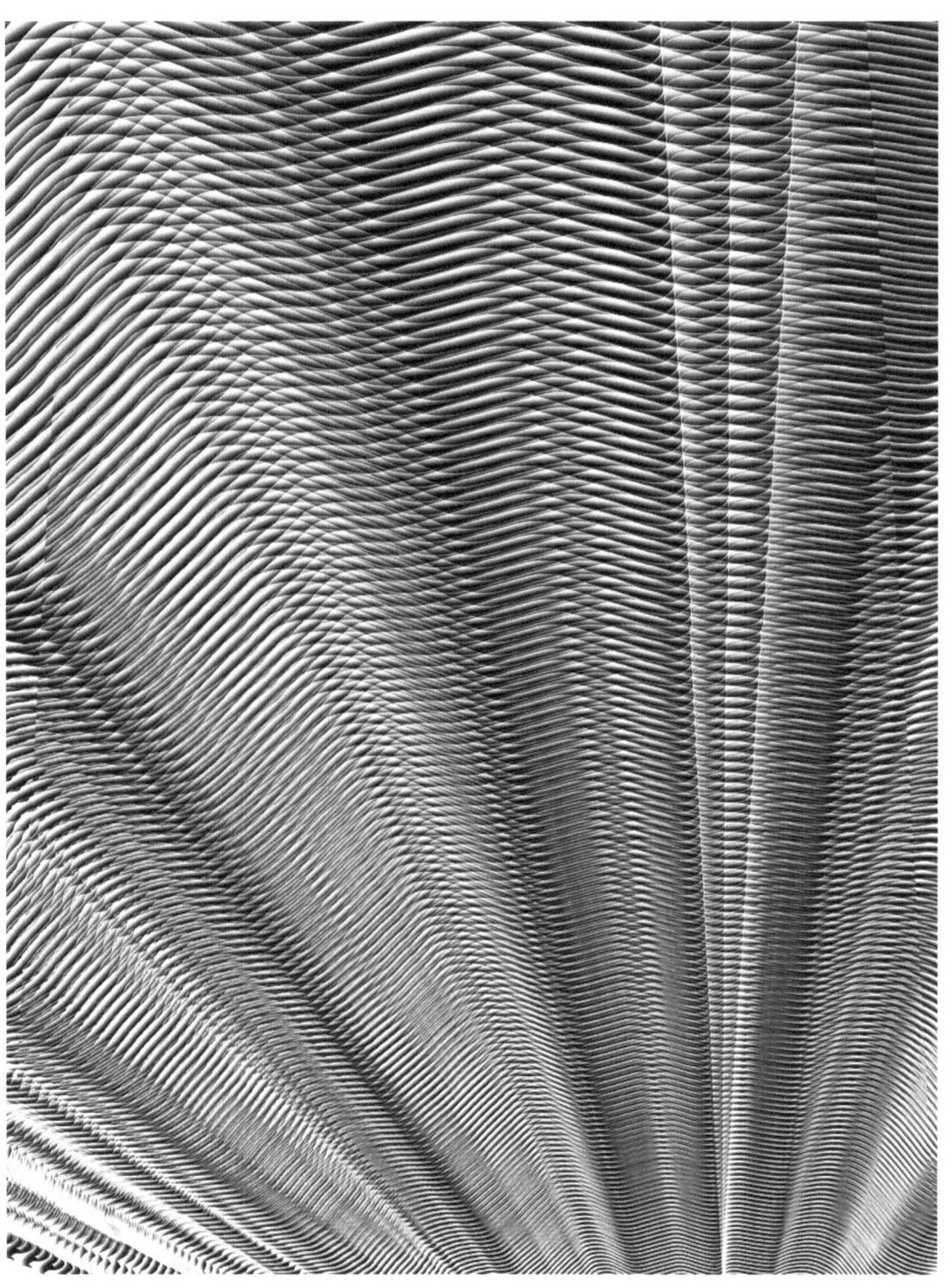

Tall Tilted – D2 Blue Quad

2009,
38" x 30" Archival Print on 44" x 36" Satin Paper
Edition of 3

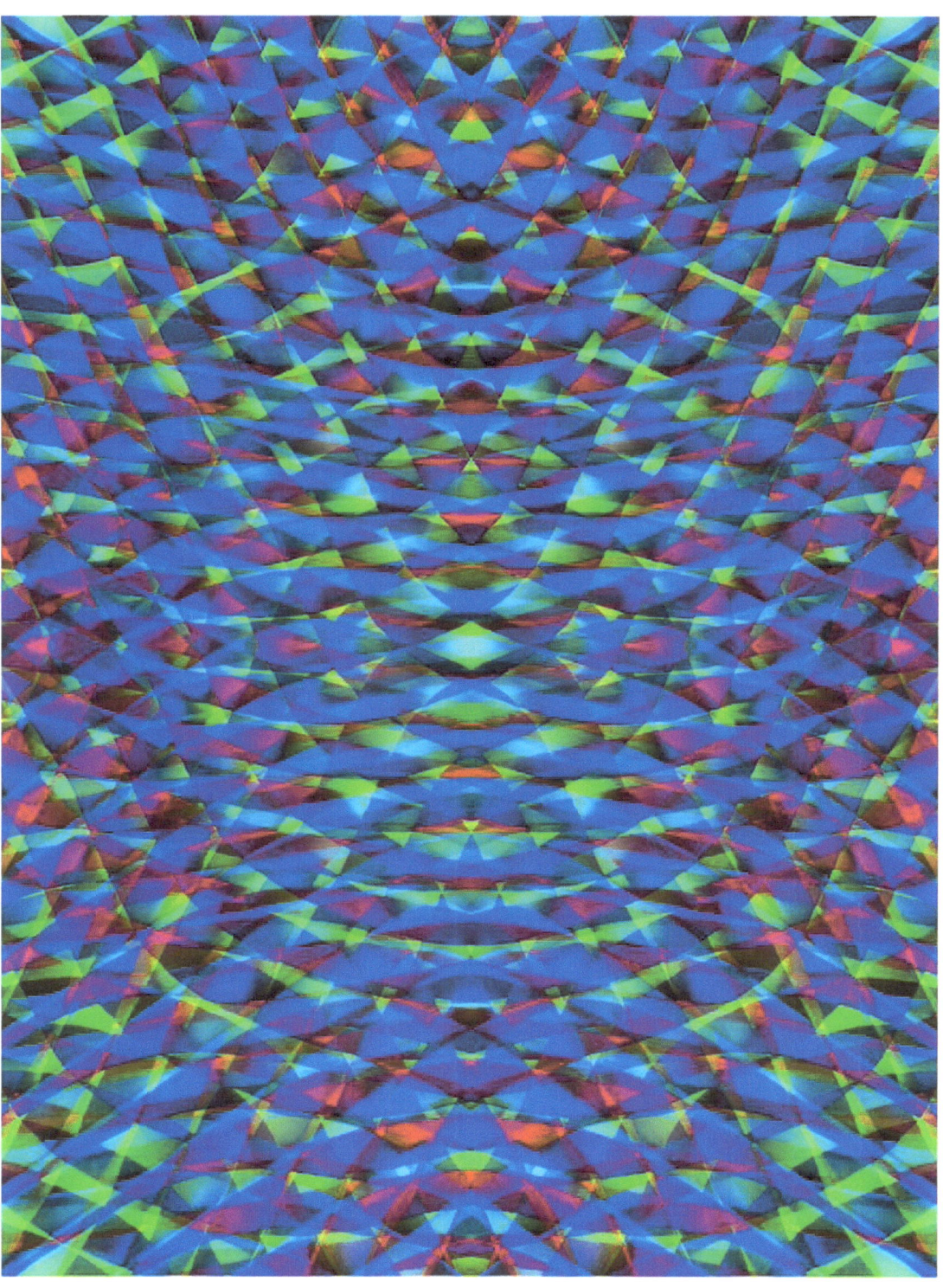

Tall Tilted – D1 Blue

2009,
38" x 30" Archival Print on 44" x 36" Satin Paper
Edition of 3

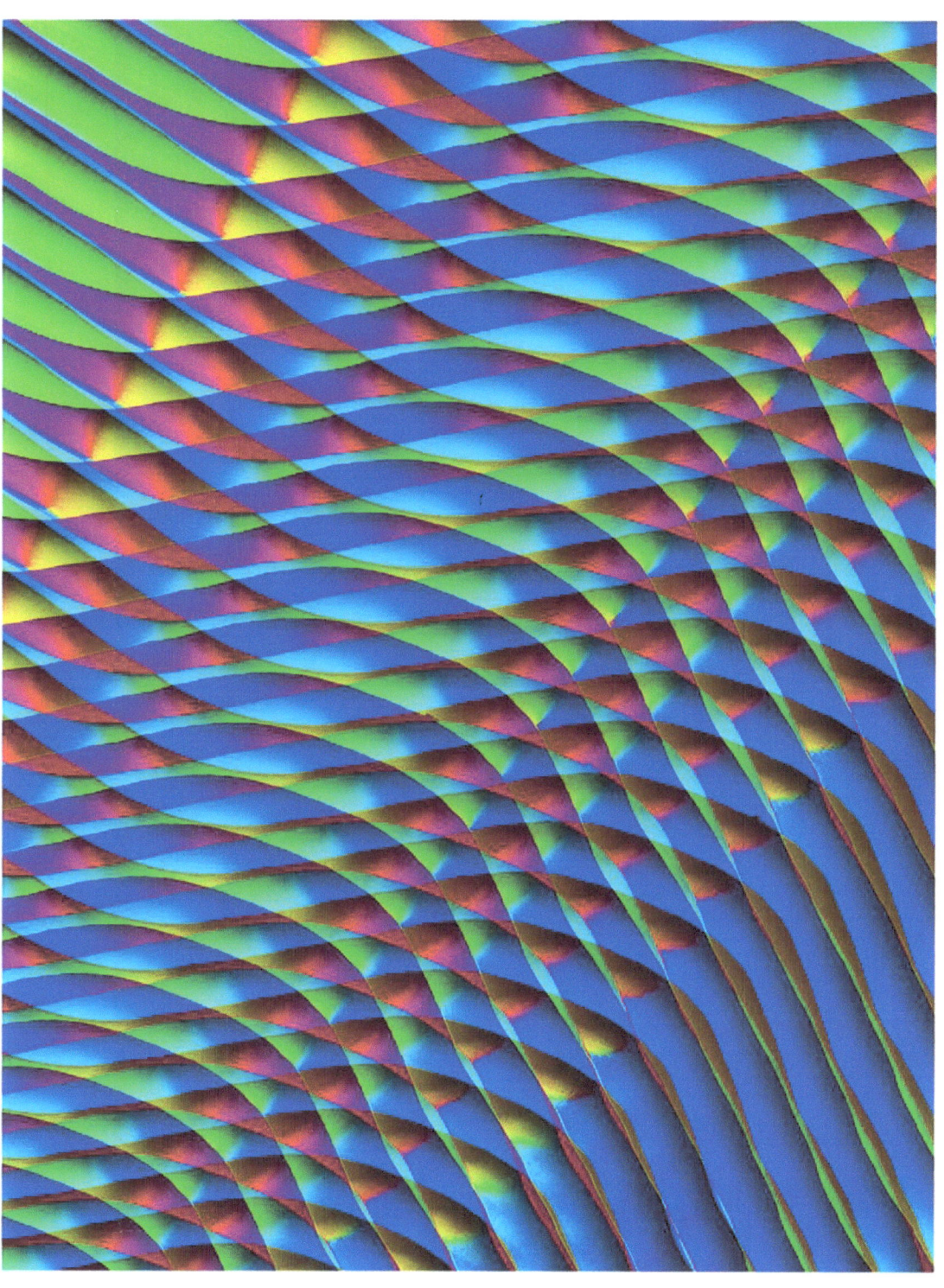

Tall Tilted #3C

2009,
38" x 30" Archival Print on 44" x 36" Satin Paper
Edition of 3

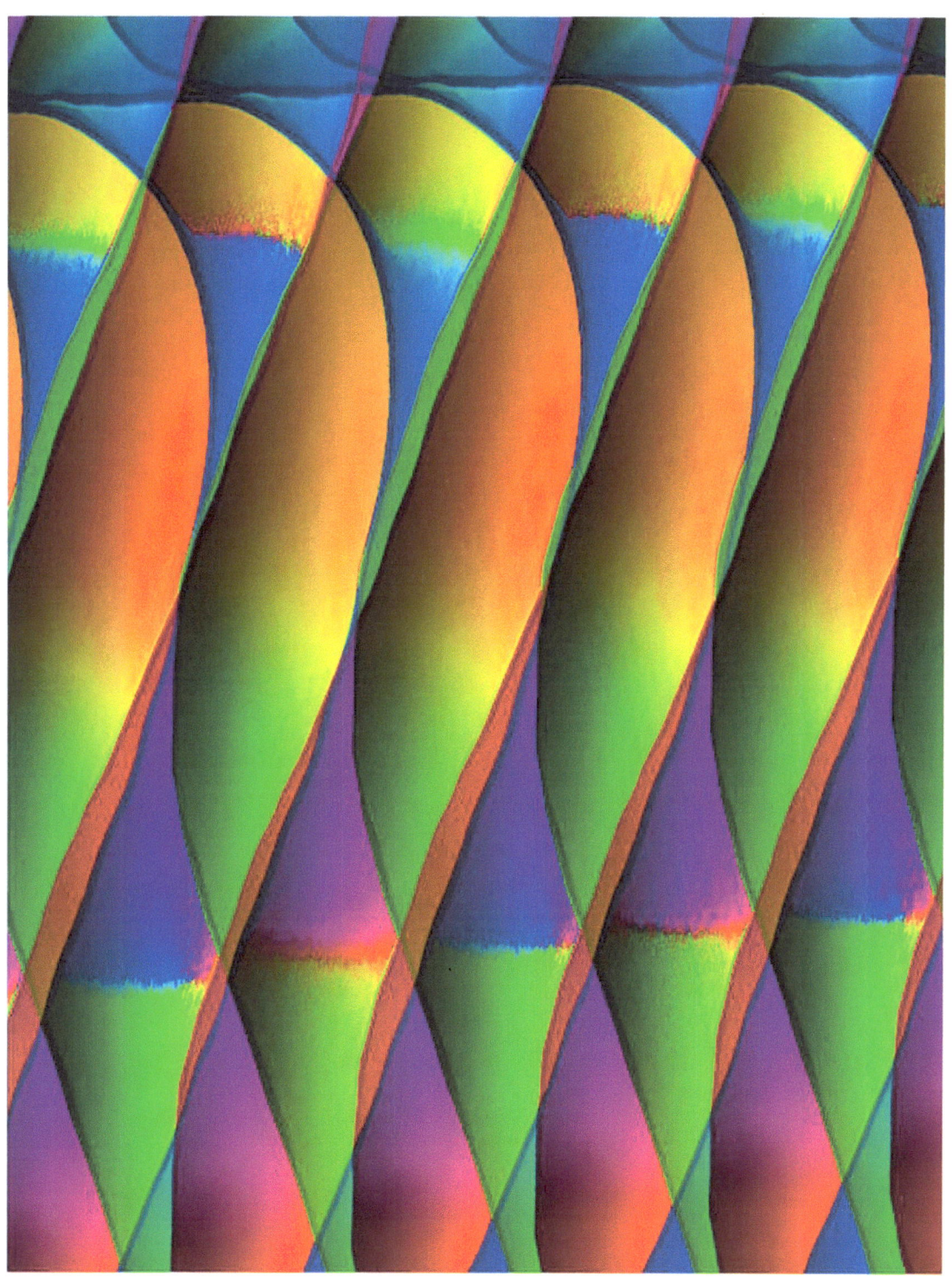

Tall Tilted #3C Doubled–B Blue

2009,
38" x 30" Archival Print on 44" x 36" Satin Paper
Edition of 3

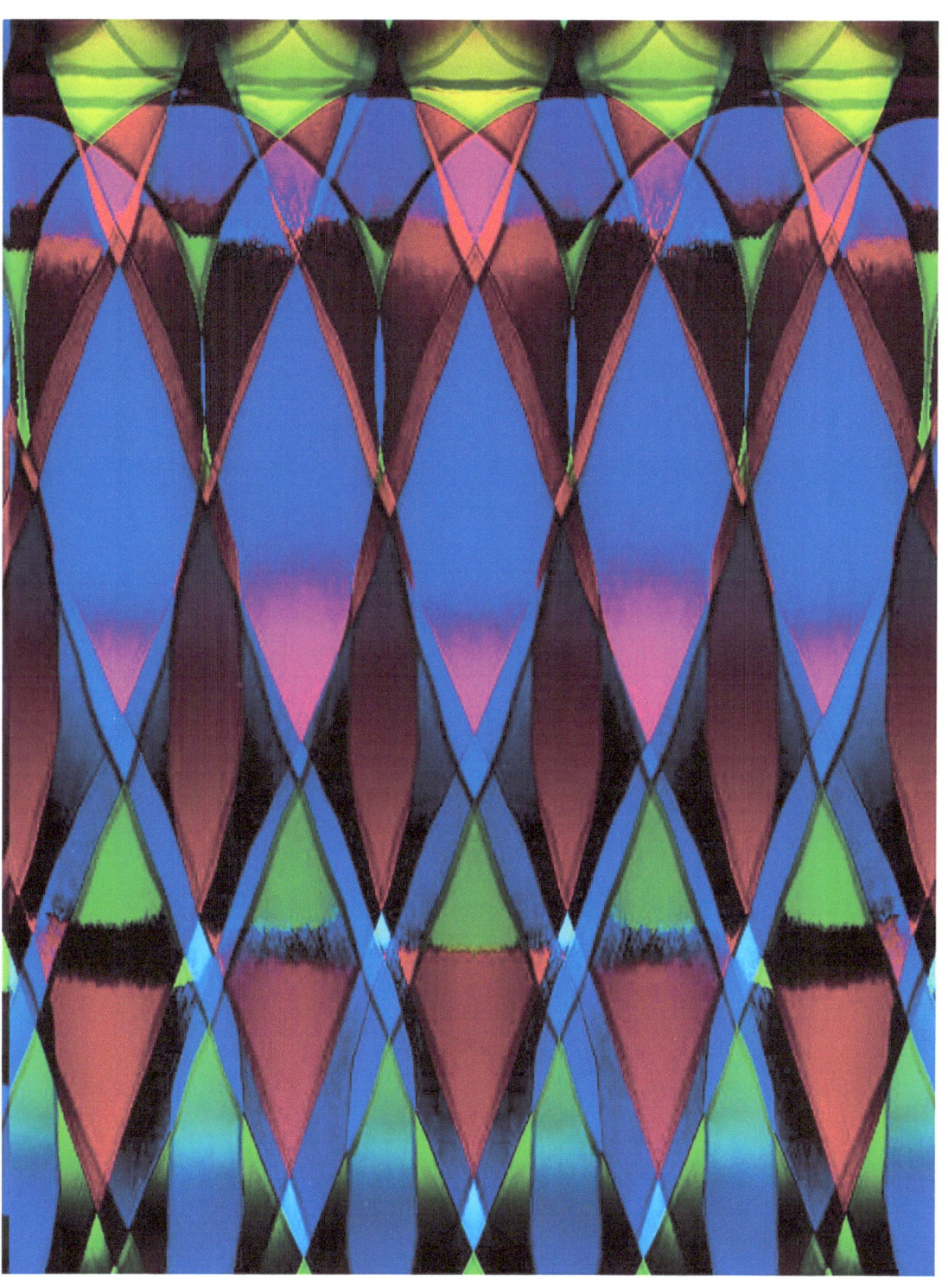

Red Leaves

2009,
38" x 30" Archival Print on 44" x 36" Satin Paper
Edition of 3

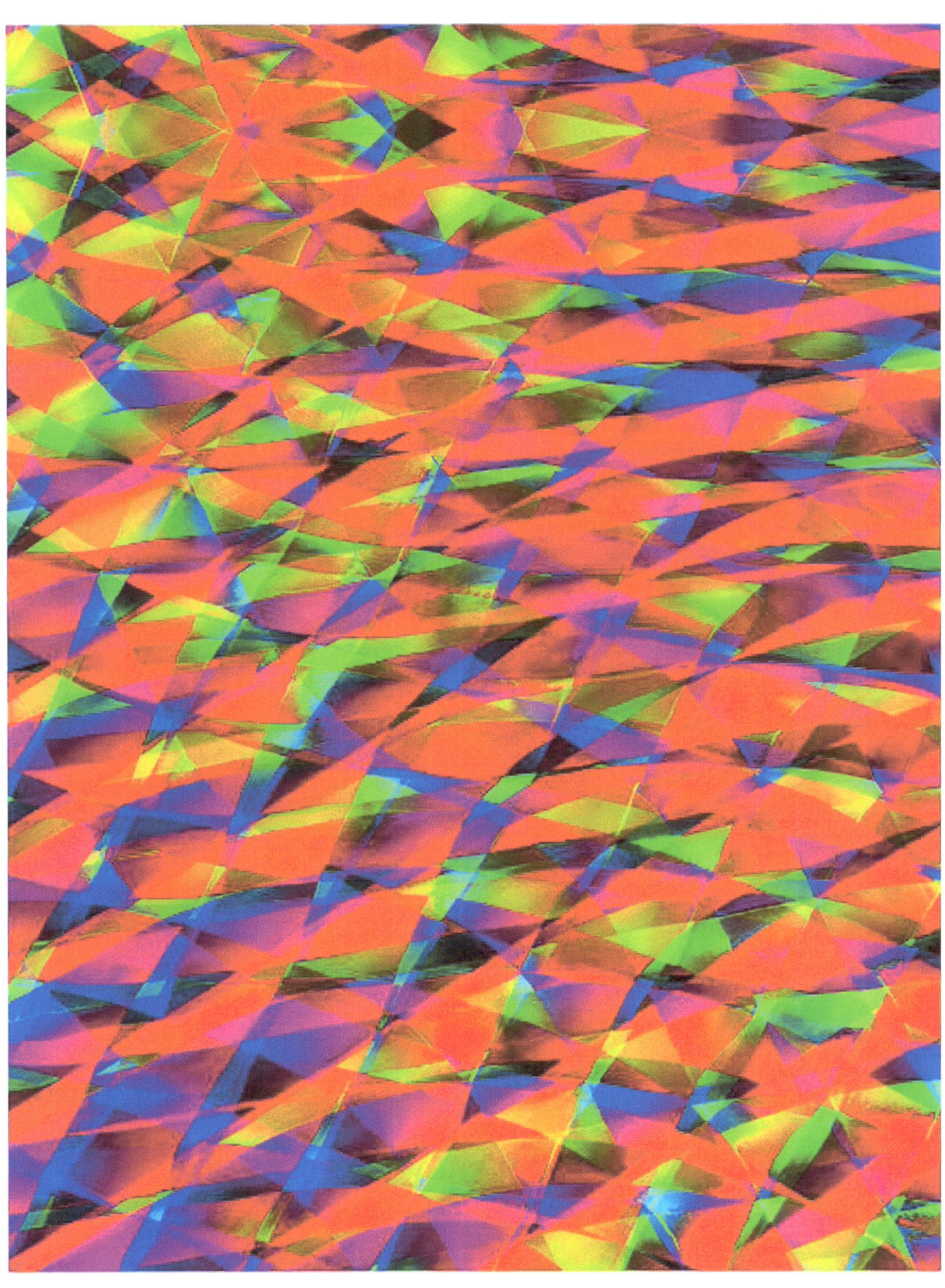

Red Point

2009,
38" x 30" Archival Print on 44" x 36" Satin Paper
Edition of 3

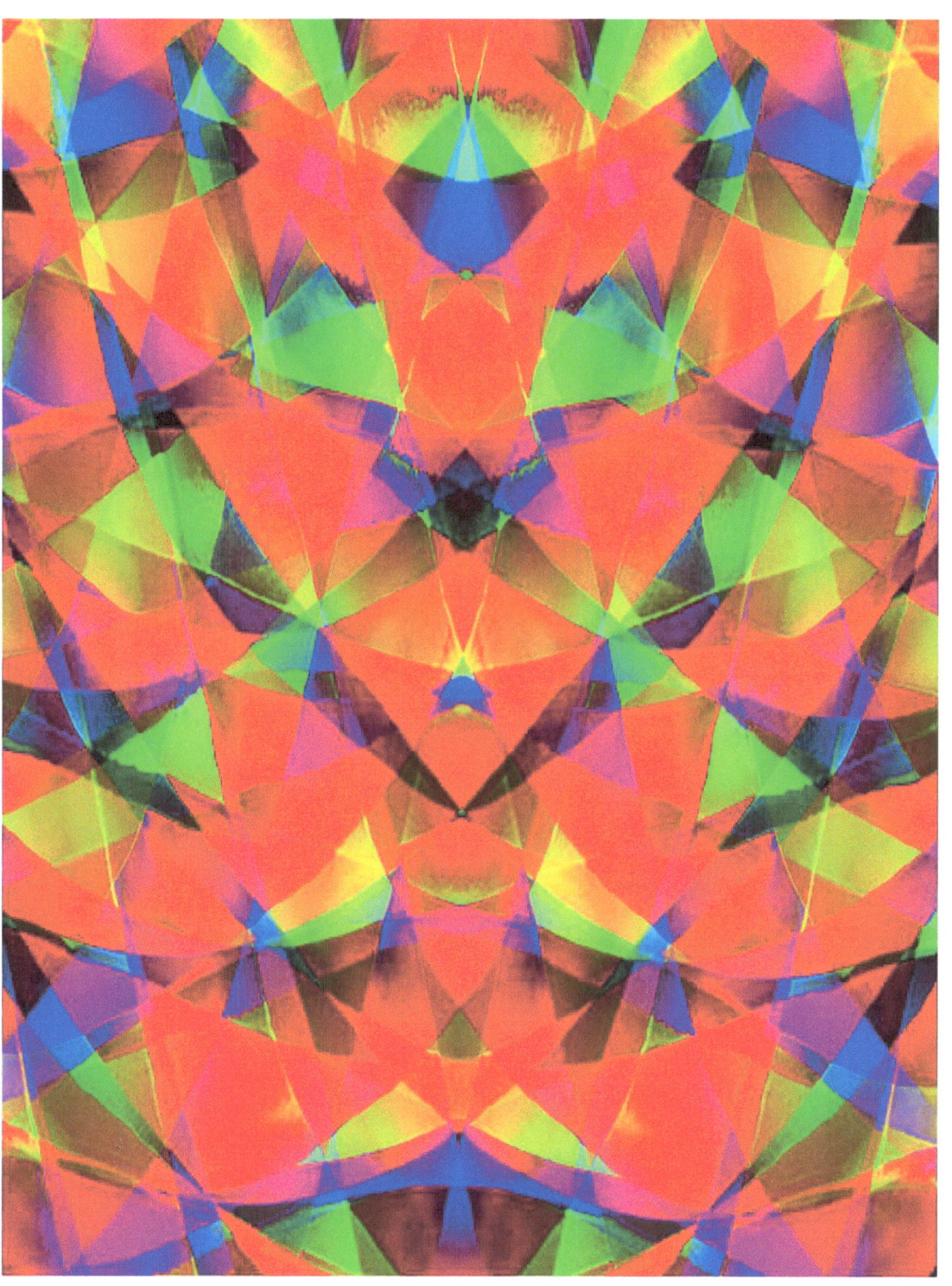

Vanishing #2

2009,
38" x 30" Archival Print on 44" x 36" Satin Paper
Edition of 3

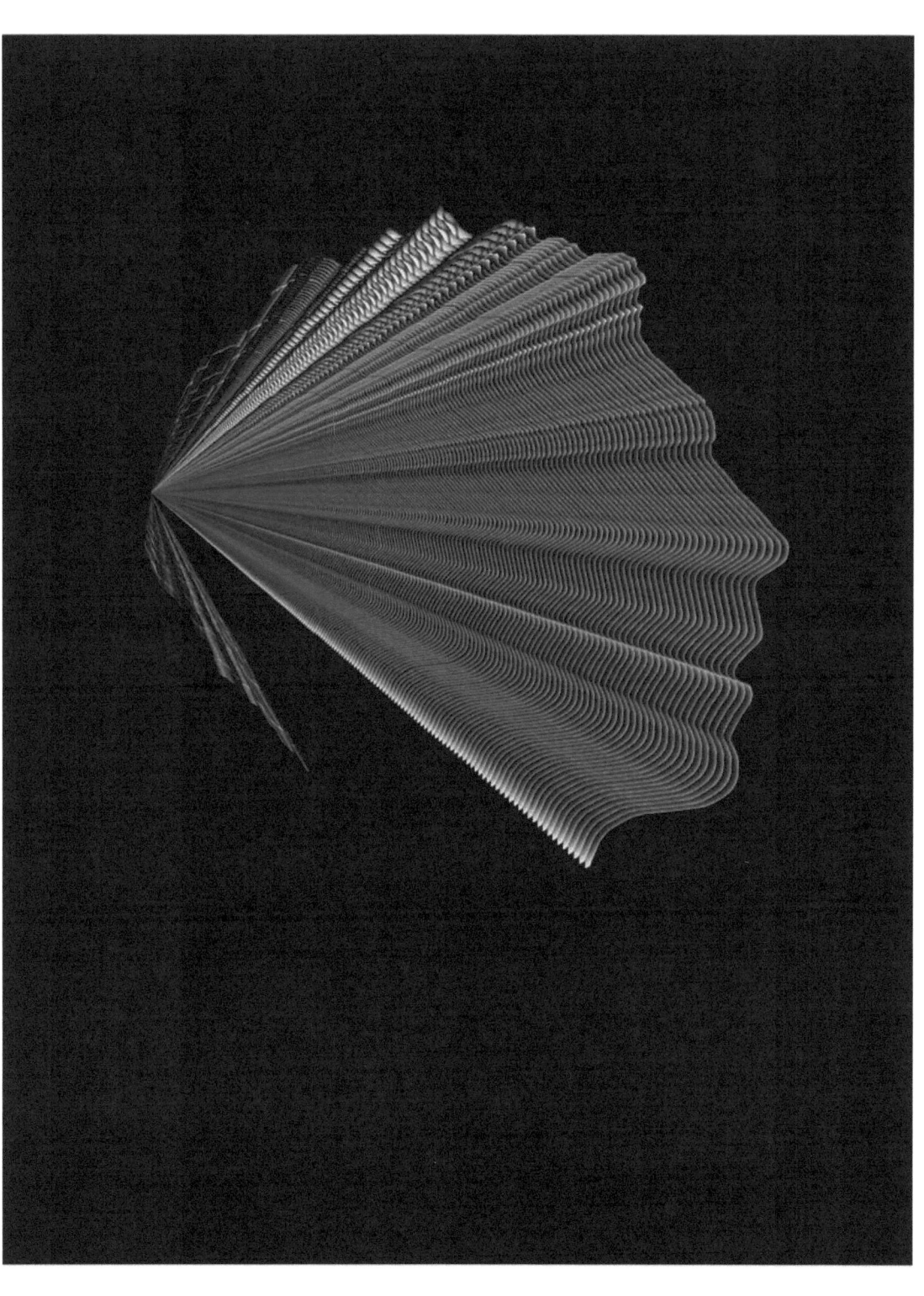

Artist's Statement

I first conceived of the Vanishing Diptych as a big hanging – to be made by creating an outline of a profile from a silhouette of a head and then shrinking that line and superimposing it upon the original over and over again to create a series of ever smaller images shrinking to a point. I then realized that the textures that made up the parts of the image were very interesting and turned many smaller areas of the original into pictures in their own right. This produced a series of images including "Tall", "Mysterious", and the "Tower" series. When I overlapped these images on transparant layers in Photoshop, I found novel interactions and even Moiré patterns, such as "Tall Tilted" and the "Difference" series. I colored the "Tower" images to produce the brilliant colors of the "Color Band" series. Coloring and overlapping differently colored layers and entire images created a large variety of colors and patterns, shown here in the derivatives of the "Tall" and the "Tall Tilted" images.

Wally Gilbert

Solo Exhibitions:

"Vanishing," BAAK Gallery, Cambridge, MA, October 15 – November 11, 2009

"Ballet Silhouette Images," Brite Smile, Beverly Hills, CA, July 24 – Sept 25, 2009

Norblin Installation, Poznan, Poland, curated by Jan Kubasiewicz and Zuk Piekowski, May 11 – 22, 2009

"Boston Ballet & Beyond," Schomburg Gallery, Santa Monica, CA, May 9 – June 6, 2009

"Stillness and Motion Images," Brite Smile, Beverly Hills, CA, May 8 – June 8, 2009

"The Norblin Project and other Images," CJ Art Gallery, San Diego, CA, May 7, 2009

"IN COLOR & BEYOND," Khaki Gallery, Boston, MA, April 14 – May 30, 2009

"Fresh Fruit," Mayyim Hayyim Gallery, Newton, MA, April – June, 2009

"Nine Ballet Images," Brite Smile, Beverly Hills, CA, February 16 – April 27, 2009

"Stillness and Motion," Audis Husar Fine Art, Beverly Hills, CA, October 10 – November 28, 2008

"Stillness and Motion," Viridian Artists, Chelsea, NYC, September 2 – 27, 2008

"LEEKS & CHAINS," Khaki Gallery, Wellesley, MA, April 22 – May 30, 2008

"The Norblin Project and other Images," CJ Art Gallery, San Diego, CA, November 1 – November 29, 2007

BAAK Gallery, Cambridge, MA, October 18 – November 14, 2007

Norblin Installation, Galeria PATIO, Lodz, Poland, curated by Zuk Piekowski, Jan Kubasiewicz,
        and Aurelia Mandziuk, September 1 – October 14, 2007

Norblin Site Installation, Warsaw, Poland, curated by Jan Kubasiewicz and Zuk Piekowski,
        May 28 – July 31, 2007

"The Norblin Project: Images of Decay," The American Center for Physics, College Park, MD,
        April – September, 2007

"IN COLOR," Khaki Gallery, Wellesley, MA, April 2 – May 10, 2007

"The Norblin Project: Images of Decay," Los Angeles Center for Digital Art, Los Angeles, CA,
        October 25 – December 9, 2006

"The Norblin Project: Images of Decay," Viridian Artists, Chelsea, NYC, September 26 – October 14, 2006

Jock Colville Hall, Churchill College, University of Cambridge, Cambridge, UK, June 13 – 25, 2006

BAAK Gallery, Cambridge, MA, February 8 – 28, 2006

Cold Spring Harbor Laboratory, Cold Spring Harbor, NY, August, 2005

Cold Spring Harbor Public Library, Cold Spring Harbor, NY, September, 2005

Ann Janss Gallery, Los Angeles, CA, January – November, 2005

SCAT gallery, Somerville, MA, February 1 – March 31, 2005

Doran Gallery, Massachusetts College of Art, Boston, MA, curated by Jan Kubasiewicz,
        October 13 – November 3, 2004

Wally Gilbert is represented by:

Amy Delaporte
Art Client Services
1112 Montana Avenue, Suite 800
Santa Monica, California   90403
tel./fax: 310-451-4346
http://www.artclientservices.com

CJ Art Gallery
343 4th Avenue, San Diego, CA 92101
tel. 619.595.0048   fax. 619.595.0512

Khaki Gallery
460 Harrison Avenue, Boston, MA 02118
9 Crest Road, Wellesley, MA 02482
tel. 781-237-1095   tel. 781-572-7263

Viridian Artists
530 W 25th Street, #407
New York, NY 10001
tel. 212-414-4040

www.ingramcontent.com/pod-product-compliance
Lightning Source LLC
Chambersburg PA
CBHW050743180526
45159CB00003B/1327